I0804576

HELP! I WANT TO MODEL SUBMISSION IN MARRIAGE

Glenda Hotton

Consulting Editor: Dr. Paul Tautges

Help! I Want to Model Submission in Marriage

ISBN
Paper: 978-1-63342-060-1
ePub: 978-1-63342-061-8
Mobi: 978-1-63342-062-5

Published by **Shepherd Press**
P.O. Box 24
Wapwallopen, PA 18660

www.shepherdpress.com

All Scripture is from The New American Standard Version, The Lockman Foundation, 1995.

Printed in Colombia

Designed by **documen**

Contents

INTRODUCTION

As a counselor, in preparation for writing this mini-book, I surveyed over one hundred single women, wives, homemakers, and profess-ional businesswomen to examine their definitions of submission. I think their replies are insightful and helpful so I have scattered them throughout to encourage your heart as we consider what it means to model biblical submission in marriage.[1]

> *Submission is the privilege of living my life according to the Lord's plan and purpose for relationships. Its practice is an act of loving obedience to the Lord's commandments regarding our relationship with our spouses ... My honor to the Lord may be measured by the submission I show my husband. This act of submission does not mean that I am inferior to my husband in any way,*

intellectually or spiritually. I am simply lining up under the authority ...

(HD)

We'll explore this in more depth in the next chapter, but for now let's acknowledge that submission can be challenging at times.

"I can't do this any longer. Why do I have to submit to him?" The woman sitting across from me was broken and confused. In her marriage, she felt that her opinions didn't count, her ideas were made fun of, and she had to ask her husband for the smallest amount of money that she wanted to spend. It just didn't seem fair.

Other wives come to me sincerely wanting to understand the biblical command to submit to their husbands. They are often confused about what submission requires and ask, "Shouldn't he have to earn my respect and submission?" So, what is true biblical submission? How does a strong woman learn to submit?

Maybe you have come to the place in your marriage where you have lost all desire to submit to your husband. Others seem to be able to have a good attitude about it, so you ask, "Why can't my husband be like hers?"

My heart aches for you. When I married, I didn't have a clue what submission meant. I read any and every book I could find or that anyone recommended on the subject in an effort to get along with this "difficult man." From the looks of things today, we as a Christian culture are not doing a good job of preparing our young people for godly submission in marriage. If you entered your marriage prepared for godly submission, you are more the exception than the rule. Newlyweds are as confused and misguided now as I was when I married.

Unfortunately, the world's idea of a submissive wife is distorted, humorous at best. You've seen the world's image—daily newspaper under her arm, a cup of coffee in one hand and slippers in the other, approaching her man who is sitting in a soft leather chair with his feet propped up on a stool, shoes off, waiting for his slippers and paper so he can relax before dinner. All day long she has cleaned house, cooked dinner, supervised the children, driven them to and from their various activities, met with angry neighbors, shopped in crowded stores, and fought the battle at the bank. She too might enjoy sitting in a soft chair and resting before dinner!

Do you feel as if you fit into that picture?

Most wives have been challenged at one time or another with the issue of submitting to their own husbands. Yes, it can be a struggle even for those who appear to have the perfect husband.

In our journey together we will look at how God's idea of submission works, define what it means and what it does not mean, consider its implications in marriage, dispel some lies, and end with some practical helps for application.

It is my prayer that as we ponder this topic we will begin to understand that it is God's plan for a husband to protect his wife and give her the freedom to be the special person she was created to be as she submits to his leadership. Through choosing to trust God, and submitting to his design for men and women, marriage can be joy unspeakable and full of glory.

> *There is never peace in the home when a contentious woman has placed herself at the head of it. Peace and harmony, both in the marriage relationship and in the home, can only be achieved when a wife surrenders to God and obeys his command to submit to the authority of her own husband.*
>
> *(MFA)*

1 Me, Submit? To Him?

I was raised in a single-parent family in which independence was encouraged. As the firstborn, it was natural for me to assert the leadership role. The surprise came when I married and my husband wanted to be the leader in our home. The first time he said no to one of my plans, or suggested we do something a different way, I thought, "Who are you to tell me what to do? Submit? I don't think so!"

It wasn't long before my independence was causing my marriage to fall apart. I was hindering my husband from being the leader God created him to be. I didn't have a clue what it meant to follow his lead, much less to submit. But as I grew to love the Lord with all my heart, mind, and soul, I learned to entrust him with my marriage. I joined a Titus 2 Bible study group[2] and learned from older women who had been where I was. I made a decision to submit to my husband and trust God.

This is not to say that trusting God with our

husband, or our marriage, is easy. It certainly is not! There are many difficult situations wives find themselves in, but God's truth gives us the guidance we need to navigate wisely and in a manner that honors the Lord.

Judy[3] had been married seventeen years when she came into my office. I recognized the symptoms of wife abuse immediately, but waited to hear her story. I have heard her type of story hundreds of times, but without fail I cry with each account. Her husband is a leader in their church and community. On the outside she is the epitome of the sweet submissive wife who stands beside her husband through thick and thin. When her husband found out she had gone to their pastor for help, he was furious and became more abusive—threatening her life if she ever embarrassed him like that again. He told her that if she thought he was abusive, it was her fault for not being more submissive. Judy had had enough. Although hesitant to talk, she came for help.

The counsel Judy needed was undoubtedly difficult for her to hear and follow. With the information given, this appeared to be a situation where there was risk of physical harm to Judy (and her children?). Especially in light of her husband's position in the church, she was advised to return to her pastor, who would hopefully view this as a serious matter and begin working through the situation biblically with Judy and her husband. Perhaps Judy also needed to consider removing herself temporarily from this volatile situation with the goal of reconciling the marriage through counseling for both her and her husband.

Carol, a prominent Christian physician's wife, reported verbal abuse so demeaning that she had come to believe her husband's remarks that she was a horrible Christian, an unloving wife, and could do nothing right. She reminded me of a squashed potato bug: no substance left. She couldn't smile or lift her head to look me in the eye. Hesitantly, in broken sentences, she shared her story. Her husband blamed her for his outbursts, stating that they resulted from her lack of submission.

In Carol's situation, she would benefit from being discipled by an older woman in her church who could lead her to see, through the Scriptures, who she is in Christ. Her husband's lack of control over his anger is not her fault unless she is provoking the anger. Even if that is the case, they are each responsible before the Lord for their own sin. Both should seek counseling. Carol needs counseling in order to come to a biblical understanding of what submission is, and her husband needs counseling in order to understand what loving leadership in the home is supposed to look like, and then work toward that goal.

Sue wanted to choose homeschooling for her four early-school-aged children. Why should she consult her non-Christian husband who seemed only vaguely interested in the children's schooling? When she asked him about any other matter, he always replied, "Do whatever you want." Therefore, didn't she have the freedom to make this decision?

Sue should not simply assume her husband will agree. Therefore, out of respect for her husband's leadership role in the family, she needed to consult with him about this significant decision. Perhaps he would agree with homeschooling the children. However, if he did not agree, she needed to follow his lead. Perhaps this would be an opportunity to win her husband without a word as he saw her respectful response to him (1 Peter 3:12).

Carrie doesn't like the instructions her father left for her mom to carry out. Standing in the hall with her hands on her hips, she stamped her foot and states at a tone just below a scream, “Do you always agree with everything Daddy says?” As a mom, what is Carol to do?

This is an excellent teaching moment with Carrie’s daughter. She should answer her daughter’s question: “Of course I don’t always agree with everything Daddy says, but God has given him the leadership role in our family. He and I will discuss this privately. We usually are able to work through things until we are both in agreement. However, if we can’t, I choose to be obedient to God’s Word and it calls me to rest under Daddy’s leadership. It may not always be easy, but God’s way is always best.”

Karla has lost respect for her husband, who has become obese and harsh in his words about money, the children’s behavior, and her housekeeping and cooking. Basically the home feels like a “den of vipers” waiting to devour her at any turn. Recognizing that her yelling and critical retorts defending her place as wife, mother, and homemaker just infuriate him even more, she becomes quiet and withdrawn, developing migraines that send her to bed but give her solace and an escape from his explosions. The children choose to withdraw also, as a means of finding peace at any cost.

In this case, Karla has swung the pendulum too far in the opposite direction. Instead of shutting down completely, she needs to become a student of her husband so she'll know the best time to approach him without yelling and engaging in critical retorts toward him. She also would benefit from meeting with an older woman to discover her contribution to her difficult situation, and to come to a correct understanding of biblical submission.

> *Submission means that I show honor and respect to my husband as he serves me in his God-ordained role as head of our family before the Lord. And that I prayerfully offer my input while trusting God to direct my husband in the way we should go.*
>
> *(SS)*

The above true accounts illustrate how sincerely challenging submission is for wives. Even in the best of marriages it is against our natural inclination as wives to submit. It is our frail, fragile, and depraved nature to want to control our lives and to be accountable to no one.

In Romans 14:12, the apostle Paul says we will

each one day give an account of ourselves to God. Husbands and wives. Singles. Sons and daughters. Everyone. It's not a pop quiz if we know it's coming! So, what does the Bible say about submission? How can I live my life in preparation for giving an account to God?

It is important that we understand what submission means, but equally important that we understand what it does not mean. Many women tend to believe that if they submit to their husband, it will mean that they are inferior to him, they are paying for Eve's sin, they may never express any ideas or opinions, or use their talents and abilities. Whatever it means, it definitely doesn't fit with the lifestyles of the five women mentioned. Nor does it reflect their desires for their future. In each of those cases a biblical understanding of what submission is, and is not, will clarify their situations. If you are in an abusive situation, I urge you to consult *HELP! Someone I Love Has Been Abused* for further help and resources. Pastor and counselor Jim Newheiser writes, "There is never an excuse for physical, verbal, emotional or sexual abuse."[4]

Even when submission is generally understood, Christian women learn very early that living in accord with the biblical teaching on submission is a most unpopular thing to do among women today. Christian homes are to reflect an image that represents God's example of a marriage, yet statistics tell us that just as many Christian marriages end in divorce as do non-Christian marriages.[5] How sad!

Submission Is ...

An Attitude Before It Is an Action

It is a belief that it is God's best for the marriage. It is actively expressing faith in God's Word and his motives in giving us this command.

A Command

Some wives think of only the Old Testament's instructions as commands. But in the New Testament, Jesus said much about obeying his commands out of love for Him:

> *If you love Me, you will keep My commandments.*
>
> (John 14:15; see also John 14:21; 1 John 2:3–4)

If a woman is not convinced that the principle of submission is God's command, she will be swayed by the unscriptural advice the world has to offer. The world's advice changes almost daily, as soon as a new article or book is written.

Submission is God's command, and God is the one a woman obeys when she submits to her husband. That adds a whole new dimension. It promotes a proper attitude, and transforms obedience into submission. The wife, when obeying her husband, will say first to herself, "Yes, Lord," then "Yes, Dear."[6]

> *Submission is willingly, cheerfully, and respectfully coming under the umbrella of my husband's protective authority. Not demanding my own way, but discussing situations with my husband and allowing him to make the final decision. There can't be any begrudging or I-told-you-so attitude for it to be true submission, but a quiet, gentle, encouraging spirit. Recognizing that God has placed him as the head/leader of the home, and purposely trying not to usurp his power, but to be a helpmate or helper suitable for what my husband needs. Doing him good and not evil all the days of our lives.*
>
> *(CD)*

When a woman submits in this manner it gives her freedom to become all that she desires and dreams of, because first she is submitting to the Lord.

Submission Is Not ...

Being a Doormat

God has not given men permission to be inconsiderate of their wives or in any way to abuse them. He has not told men to do things that will be hazardous to their wives' mental and emotional health. Remember, the command to wives to submit to their husbands is followed by the command to husbands to love their wives as Christ loved the church and gave his life for her (Ephesians 5:25).

Men and women are different. But not all women believe that is how God ordained it. Their thinking comes out of the teaching of the current women's liberation movement, which tells us that we have been sex-role socialized. It is taught in our secular universities that we have been programmed since childhood how to act and behave as women, thus creating a sense of inferiority. God says we are not inferior but equal in all ways. Equal but different! God has given men and women different roles to play in marriage.

About Who Is Superior

The title of "leader in the home" is not one for which we can compete, to see who is best. God said, "The husband is the head of the wife" (Ephesians 5:23). God knows our strengths and weaknesses, and he uses all for his glory.

If a husband is wise, he will seek his wife's wisdom, knowledge, and opinions. But many husbands say that they cannot use their wife's talents, efficiency, or intelligence because she tends to take over.

It is easy to recognize wives who are more gifted in some areas than their husbands. Some are naturally adept at finances, creative gardening, decorating, or organizing. But statements like, "I'm more gifted with administration so I lead our family," may be extremely destructive for the husband who is trying to excel as leader in the home. However, I want to add that a man who is confident and secure in his role of leader in the home may recognize that his wife is gifted in such areas and may ask her to take those responsibilities. He will be proud of her help. Taking on these roles in this manner still constitutes submission.

Being Passive

Some women are naturally quiet and give their input very carefully, and by nature find it a challenge. If a wife, however, withholds her input because of fear or desiring peace at all costs, this is not submission. Yet there are times when a wife will choose to be quiet for a purpose—a bigger plan.

Jesus, God in the flesh, is our example in all things, and in Mark 15:3–5 he gives an example of being quiet with a purpose:

> *The chief priests began to accuse Him harshly. Then Pilate questioned Him again, saying, "Do You not answer? See how many charges they bring against You!" But Jesus made no further answer; so Pilate was amazed.*

Christ was not afraid to say something. He was not afraid to defend himself. He was not terrified of what Pilate would do. He knew what Pilate could do and knew he didn't have to defend himself because God had a bigger plan. He was still in charge, but he didn't waste his words by defending himself. When a woman holds her voice for a season, it gives her the ability to gain control of herself, to choose her words carefully, to pray and seek guidance, to journal her facts, thoughts, ideas, opinions, and intuitions, and to present all to her husband in an orderly fashion.

Although Jesus was silent, he was not passive. He was actively pursuing his goal. A woman may be in control of herself and waiting for the right moment to confront her husband with a concern. This is not being passive; this is demonstrating her strength. It may appear to an onlooker that she is passive, but in reality she is exercising intelligence, discernment, and Spirit-control by presenting her concern in private when both are calm and she is prepared.

On the other hand, a wife who chooses passivity is putting her mind in neutral—contributing nothing to the marriage relationship.

When a husband asks his wife, "What do you think about this?" he expects her to give input. She is his helpmate. She is specially created to help him become a better leader by giving her input, then submitting to his decision.

Determined By Who Is Right

Christians live within the parameters of scriptural principles and their own preferences. If Scripture has spoken on an issue, God expects us to pay attention. But some things are what we may call "gray areas" and are subject to personal preferences. Many situations that come up in a family may not have a clear scriptural right or wrong. It is important to share our preferences, but we must remember that God works through our husbands for the good of the whole family *and* that our husband will answer to God for his choices. This puts a wife in the privileged position of loving her husband by praying that God will grant him great wisdom as he leads the family.

Submission is easy when we agree with our husband's decisions. But the test comes, of course, when he chooses the opposite of what we want. This requires us to trust that God's way is the best way, and to understand that he will care for us and that true happiness comes through trusting God. He has called *every* wife to submit to her own husband. First Peter 3:1–2 says,

> *In the same way, you wives, be submissive to your own husbands so that even if any of them are disobedient to the word, they may be won without a word by the behavior of their wives, as they observe your chaste and respectful behavior.*

This was written to wives who were married to pagan men who not only were unbelievers, but were also actively participating in the worship rites of pagan gods.

By submitting to an unsaved husband, a wife hopes that he will be saved. However, salvation is God's job; ours as wives is to submit as unto the Lord.

Dan is an unsaved husband living with a transformed, godly wife. He witnessed with amazement his wife's dramatic change in her responses to his leadership after she became a Christian. One evening, while Dan and his wife were out with another couple for dinner, he became irritated and annoyed that his friend's wife was constantly belittling, correcting, and dictating to her husband on every subject. Fed up with the disruption in conversation, Dan said to his friend, "If your wife went to the church that my wife goes to, you would be the leader in your home." Dan is still not saved, but his godly wife continues to grow and experience the peace that comes because she knows she is obeying her Lord and Savior.

A Burden to Be Borne

Rather, submission is a God-given privilege and necessity in order that homes run smoothly. A woman may take on the martyr-type stance. This wife becomes a complainer, a troublemaker, and she is very disruptive to her household. She has a "Poor me!" attitude and is a poor testimony for her Christian faith. This is not godly submission.

A Tool to Use When a Wife Wants Something

Submission comes with no strings attached. It is a desire to please God and do what is best for the family. Most women desire the inner peace that comes from living in harmony with their husbands and obeying God.

As I write this, words of a hymn by Fanny J. Crosby play in my mind:

> *Perfect submission, all is at rest,*
> *I in my Savior am happy and blest;*
> *Watching and waiting, looking above,*
> *Filled with his goodness, lost in his love.*
> *This is my story, this is my song;*
> *Praising my Savior all the day long!*[7]

Christ is our example in all things. He submitted himself, in obedience to his Father, to die on the cross as the one and only acceptable sacrifice for our sins. In Matthew 27:27–50 we find the account of his betrayal, abuse, agony, and finally his death.

He endured God's wrath against sin and was raised to new life three days later. He did this for you and me, so that we could have abundant life.

In Hebrews 12:2 we are reminded to keep our eyes on Jesus. He endured the cross, despising the shame, and now is with his Father. If you do not know him, turn to him by faith today. It is Christ who gives us the strength to endure and the peace to enjoy.

If you do not know Christ as your Lord and Savior, it will be almost impossible to have an attitude of submission to your husband and to trust God to work in your marriage.

Ask your pastor or elder in your church to introduce you to this wonderful loving God, who loves you (Romans 5:6–10). He loves you so much that he gave his only Son to die on the cross—a miserable death—for you, and raised him from the dead so that you may have spiritual life and rest. Jesus says,

> *Come to Me, all who are weary and*
> *heavy-laden, and I will give you rest.*
> (Matthew 11:28)

The blessed assurance that submission brings is a fruit of a Christian's faith.

In John 10:10, Christ says that he came to give "life ... abundantly":

> *The thief comes only to steal and kill and destroy; I came that they may have life, and have it abundantly.*

The abundant life is not a problem-free life of continually happy circumstances; it is a life of overcoming temptations and trials with the wisdom and strength that Jesus gives. God wants his children to be full of the joy of Christ.

It is grievous when a woman reaches the place in her marriage where she feels that she absolutely cannot and will not submit to a harsh and thoughtless man—the one to whom she has given her heart and who promised to love and cherish her "till death do us part." She may go so far as to see no way out until death separates them. This is not the abundant life Jesus brings. So, what happened?

2 Understanding the Difficulty of Submission

Back in the Garden of Eden, when Eve stepped away from the protection of Adam to eat the fruit forbidden by God, and when Adam stepped down from his leadership role by letting Eve talk him into participating, the upheaval of God's design took place (Genesis 3). That sin nature has come to all of us through Adam. The Bible says,

> *Therefore, ... through one man sin entered into the world, and death through sin, and so death spread to all men, because all sinned.*
>
> (*Romans 5:12*)

Add to our sinful nature the cultural influences of feminism and "equality of the sexes," and we see that God's design for marriage continues to be sabotaged by role reversal.

The root, heart issue is not really submission to just our husbands: it is submission in general. If we took out God's command to wives to submit to their husbands, we'd still have to deal with his command to "be subject to one another in the fear of Christ" (Ephesians 5:21). And consider Philippians 2:3–7a,

> *Do nothing from selfishness or empty conceit, but with humility of mind regard one another as more important than yourselves; do not merely look out for your own personal interests, but also for the interests of others. Have this attitude in yourselves which was also in Christ Jesus, who, although He existed in the form of God, did not regard equality with God a thing to be grasped, but emptied Himself ...*

I don't know about you, but *that's* hard enough for me to do! Do I daily empty myself? Or do I daily grasp at equality? Am I fighting for my rights, or am I daily, moment by moment, enjoying the privilege of laying them down, in love?

"But you don't know my husband!" you say. God does. And he said to Peter, who was concerned about God's plan for the apostle John, "If I want him to remain until I come, what is that to you?

You follow Me!" (John 21:22). Ouch! God wants to work in me. Of course, God wants to grow my husband too, but he'd likely say that's not my concern.

The Principle of Submission

I am often reminded of the meaning of submission when another person and I arrive at a door at the same time. One of us steps back and gestures for the other to enter first. There isn't room for both to enter the door together, so one of us submits to the other.

The principle of submission is generally recognized in society. In every area of life the most efficient way of operation is in a line of authority, with each person doing his or her share to get the job done. The governments of many countries operate through authoritative heads—the president, prime minister, chancellor, king, or queen—with most of the working authority delegated to others. Those working under the authority are expected to willingly and without threat of force submit themselves to the law.

Church leadership also involves submission. The minister—with elders, deacons, board members, or overseers—exercises authority. When there is a chairperson and a tie-breaking vote, the other members cooperate with the chairperson in order for all to operate efficiently. Each person performs his or her responsibilities within the sphere of authority to get the job done. Why is that? Where do the concepts of authority and submission originate?

The concept of submission originates from the structure of the relationships within the Trinity. This is critical for us to understand since it not only reveals something about God's original design for structure in marriage, but also testifies to the fact that submission does not mean one person is of lesser value than the other. Consider the following biblical teaching:

> *But I want you to understand that Christ is the head of every man, and the man is the head of a woman, and God is the head of Christ.*
>
> *(1 Corinthians 11:3)*

The fundamental principle revealed here is this: Divine order requires the subjection of some to the divinely bestowed authority of others. The word "head" incorporates authority. The Father is the head of the Son, Christ submits to the Father, and yet both are equally God. The Holy Spirit is sent out by the Father and the Son, and yet all three are equally God.

Submission in Marriage

Accordingly, the biblical teaching concerning the wife's submission to her husband is not an attack upon her worth. The wife is equal in worth before God, being also created in his image (Genesis 1:27), yet she has been created to serve God in a different manner than her husband. When God created man and woman, he created them with distinct roles in order to carry out distinct purposes. Since God is the God of order, he established authority structures that best reflect his character and nature. The woman's submission to her husband in the home is not based upon inferiority. In God's eyes, men and women are equal in worth and value, but distinct in role and function. In order for both to be completely fulfilled each must strive to fulfill his and her God-given role.

My husband and I view our marriage as a partnership—a partnership that has different roles, yet sometimes they overlap depending on circumstances. All of our

> *decisions are made together and if we can't agree, we wait it out until we have reached an understanding. A few times my husband has said, "I would like to make the final decision on that and want to take responsibility for that." He knows that he is head of the home and therefore responsible for his family and their spiritual growth.*
>
> *(JC)*

We noted earlier, in Ephesians 5, that we are all to be subject to one another in the fear of Christ. Christ has shown us a general attitude of submission that Christians are to have toward one another, receiving one another's ideas and respecting one another's efforts and accomplishments. That passage goes on,

> Wives, be subject to your own husbands, as to the Lord. For the husband is the head of the wife, as Christ also is the head of the church, He Himself being the Savior of the body. But as the church is subject to Christ, so also the wives ought to be to their husbands in everything.
>
> (Ephesians 5:22–24)

Here the instructions are specifically given to wives to be submissive to their own husbands. Submission in the home is much more than a general attitude. God's will is that a wife should submit to her own husband—not to just any man—and that she will do this as unto the Lord with a godly attitude. Submission is a choice each of us must make, daily.

> *In my marriage, submission means that after my husband and I discuss something we need to make a decision about, from the color of the carpet in the living room, how and where we spend money, to the way we handle a discipline issue with a child—if we disagree, his word is the final decision. I am submitting to his authority as husband and head of our household.*
>
> *(HE)*

A look at Scripture reveals that God is serious about his command regarding submission. If God tells us something once, it is important. When he tells us repeatedly, we had best listen. In each of the Scriptures to wives regarding submission, it says "to your own husbands."

Wives, be subject to your own husbands, as to the Lord ... But as the church is subject to Christ, so also the wives ought to be to their husbands in everything ... And the wife must see to it that she respects her husband.

(Ephesians 5:22, 24, 33b)

Wives, be subject to your husbands, as is fitting in the Lord.

(Colossians 3:18)

In the same way, you wives, be submissive to your own husbands so that even if any of them are disobedient to the word, they may be won without a word by the behavior of their wives ... For in this way in former times the holy women also, who hoped in God, used to adorn themselves, being submissive to their own husbands.

(1 Peter 3:1, 5)

In this book, I have specifically focused on the wife's role and left out the responsibilities of the husband. His role is much weightier and he will be held accountable for the ways he fulfills God's instructions or abdicates his responsibilities. If we focus on our husband's role we tend to get frustrated by rationalizing that if he were only doing his part, ours would be so easy.

There comes a time when each of us needs to decide to get along with our husbands, not because he deserves it or because we feel like it, but because we choose to honor God and live our lives according to his will, not ours. After all, we are the ones who were created to be the helpers, not the other way around. We must make the decision to become the godly women God created us to be, regardless of what our husbands do or do not do. It is obvious that we can't change or control others; we can only change or control ourselves. So for a wife to spend her time trying to make sure her husband does his job is not a wise use of her time. It is wiser to learn how to live out our own unique role in a manner that recognizes her own accountability to God.

> *Basically, I believe submission is the willing support of a wife to her husband with a good attitude. She can and sometimes should state her own thoughts about a matter, but once he decides something, she should do her best to*

emotionally and willingly support him,
even if it means letting him fail.

(NE)

God has set up his order for the universe, the home and each spouse's role within it. Eve left us with the sinful desire to rule our husbands, but God reminds us that our husbands will be over us:

Your desire will be for your husband,
And he will rule over you.

(Genesis 3:16b)

This competition for authority is a result of the curse of sin. A wife's inborn desire to control her husband and make him serve her is a result of sin; it is not part of God's original design for marriage.

Submission to Our Husband's God-Given Authority

If we read Genesis 1–3 chronologically, we notice that God established authority in the home before woman was created. He also placed inside of men five drives:

To Exercise Dominion, Rule, and Have Authority

> *Then God said, "Let Us make man in Our image, according to Our likeness; and let them rule over the fish of the sea and over the birds of the sky and over the cattle and over all the earth, and over every creeping thing that creeps on the earth."*
>
> (Genesis 1:26)

Thus man has a sense of responsibility, a competition for authority, and a desire for a defined territory. This text explains his expectation of respect in his role as leader and the confidence he needs to perform it.

To Subdue, Overcome, or Be More Powerful

> *God blessed them; and God said to them, "Be fruitful and multiply, and fill the earth, and subdue it; and rule over the fish of the sea and over the birds of the sky and over every living thing that moves on the earth."*
>
> (Genesis 1:28)

To subdue is man's willingness to accept challenges, to bring the forces of nature under his control and prove his ability to do so—his inventiveness.

To Multiply and Replenish, a Natural Sex Drive

We see this also in Genesis 1:28 (quoted above). We seem to understand this innate drive the best. But we need to remember that a man needs release regularly or it is painful for him. Sexual stimulus causes a bodily chemical reaction. Man desires emotional as well as physical expression. He has a desire for response from his wife.

To Tend, Dress, or Create His Own Space to Care For

> *Then the* Lord *God took the man and put him into the garden of Eden to cultivate it and keep it.*
>
> (Genesis 2:15)

This drive is expressed in man's desire to keep his home. It is where we see him express his personality and creativity. He has a desire for respect and a recognition of his provision and for the upkeep of his property by his wife.

To Keep, Guard, or Protect

This may also be seen in Genesis 2:15 (quoted above). Man demonstrates his sense of protectiveness of his wife and desires to provide for the future. He may lean toward strictness as he trains his children so that they will be successful as adults.

Understanding these five drives even briefly may help us begin to see the underlying motive for our husbands' behavior. We need to focus on our role to submit and let God work on him.

In this chapter, we've seen how God designed woman to correspond to the man—to be his complement, as a reflection of the complementary roles within the divine godhead. Several New Testament passages affirm this (1 Peter 3:1, 5; Colossians 3:18; Ephesians 5:22, 24, 33b; 1 Corinthians 11:3). Each reminds us that as a married woman we are to fit into our husband's ways. That means we adjust to him, learn about him—become a student of him—and never compare him with our neighbors, sisters, or friends. We are called to fit into God's particular calling and vocation for our husband's life. This is not bondage, but the blessing of true freedom!

3 God's Solution

In 1 Samuel 25 our attention is drawn to a woman named Abigail, whose example teaches us how to get along with a difficult man. Abigail lived an extraordinary life. In Herbert Lockyer's *All the Women of the Bible*, we see that Abigail was a woman who was wise, beautiful, and had brains. She didn't fly off the handle. She was known by the villagers as the good angel of Nabal's household. She was expressive and sunny, winsome and wise.[8]

Nabal her husband, however, was a man who was churlish and evil in his doings. He was harsh, rude, and brutal, a greedy, selfish, and angry man. He was a disgrace to his family, "a worthless man" (1 Samuel 25:17). He was dogged, surly and snappish, and always snarling—a cynic. His riches made him great in the world, but he was mean. He was also a drunk and a fool. This wretch of a man was likely an unbeliever who bowed his knee to the god of this world and not to the God of his fathers.

The Bible doesn't tell us why Abigail married such a fool. According to the custom of those times, marriages were man-made, the woman having little to say about the choice of a husband.

The account in 1 Samuel shows that Abigail had the ability to manage the household's affairs and that she had good judgment in the use of her resources. She used caution; she was circumspect as to the danger or risk she was facing. She was a God-centered woman who put God first in all she said and did. You would think that for a woman of such godliness God would provide an equally godly husband; what a wonderful blessing they would be in their ministry—honoring and glorifying God. But God chose to use her in another way, and by doing so demonstrated to us that we can be godly women in the midst of very difficult situations. The Christian woman would do well to recognize the challenge involved in her husband's responsibility to lead, and by encouraging him through biblical submission she actually helps him become the leader God has called him to be.

Many Christian wives are poorly taught (mixed up, at least) about true biblical submission. My heart aches for the wife who thinks she has been submissive but in reality has allowed her husband to walk all over her, openly disrespect her, and betray her trust by treating her as if she was less than his precious treasure that he promised to love as Christ loved the church. So many wives have taught their husbands how to ignore them and how to give up their leadership role, by exaggerating their husbands' failures and emphasizing what good jobs they can do without their husbands' input. But then their husbands have no sympathy when their wives' schemes fail and the wives cry for help.

Both the husband's and the wife's distorted thinking patterns about submission may develop from a corrupt and unbiblical understanding of God's design. For example, if a wife has sought her husband's advice and then laughed or mocked his contribution, he will not dare to venture out and try to give any input in the future. He learns quickly how to avoid conflict. Some develop an abusive lifestyle to protect themselves. It is a scary thing for a man to lead. His fear of failure haunts him. He looks for his wife's respect, and when it is missing, he will dread to tread again where he has already failed. Innately, he knows his responsibility is to provide, protect, care for, and tend his family. The buck stops with him and he knows he will give an account to God for the way he leads his household and those within it.

Although there is rebellion in Christian circles

regarding submission (its abuse and misuse), there coexists a growing desire to understand true biblical submission. Understanding and applying biblical teaching on submission can bring harmony and unity to a marriage, making it like no other relationship. When the married couple lives this out in the home, they demonstrate their love for Christ to their neighborhood, family, and friends—she through her graceful, joyful submission, and he through his loving, sacrificial leadership.

> *Submission—created equal with my husband, but filling different roles. I give input, but he makes the final decisions if we disagree about something ... It is such a place of comfort and safety.*
>
> *(SA)*

4 Applying the Truth of God's Word to Our Hearts

Although God's Word is filled with words of security for us as wives, although we may be familiar with many verses of Scripture, and although we have heard them and perhaps memorized most of them, we still need to be reminded of the strength and love and power God gives to us as his special women. It is a scary thing to step out for the first time and submit to "that sinner" we call our husband. But God's Word is truth, and the truth will set us free.

Sherry shared with me that, when she submitted her life to Christ as her Lord and Savior and read the verse in Ephesians that says that wives are to submit to their husbands, she thought that couldn't mean her—surely she was exempt because, after all, her husband wasn't a Christian, and he allowed her to run the home. As she studied the Bible and learned that, yes, indeed, every part of the Bible was applicable to her, she agreed that if God would show her, she would submit. She became convicted of her need to submit to her non-Christian husband in everything. She said that when she thought about what submission meant for her, all she could think of was that, since she was taller than her husband and she wore three-inch heels and towered over him, she would need to buy and wear flat shoes. She did this as an act of demonstrating outwardly what she wanted to do inwardly. We may laugh at this, but God honored her new commitment to obey in all things, even in her innocence, and little by little her husband began to notice his new wife.

She had been leading and ruling over her husband for some time, so at first when she began to take her role seriously and submit to him, it took him a while to pick up on the fact that she was responding to his requests. When he asked her to pick up his shirts from the cleaners, she acquiesced and did it. When he asked her to join him for a weekend away, she didn't dictate where they would go or when they would leave or what they would do. Instead she seemed pleased with his suggestion. He began to be more attentive and considerate of her needs and to open up and share his life with her. This non-Christian husband is Dan, whom I mentioned earlier.

It is important that we wives do not look at

submission as something to try out in the short-term and discard if we don't get immediate results. God's commands are not for us to try out to see if we like them or benefit from them, but they are for our good and his honor and glory. So when we commit to obey this command to submit to our husbands, we must make a decision to be faithful and trust God for the outcome.

Before we can trust God, and after we have surrendered our lives to him to be our Lord and Savior, as explained in Chapter 2, we must grow to know him. We get to know him by reading his Word, regularly attending a Bible-preaching local church, joining a Bible study, and spending daily time in prayer. We cannot grow by isolating ourselves from others and throwing ourselves a pity-party.

The Bible tells us that:

» God has a plan and his way is good. He is our stronghold and causes all things to work for good. "'For I know the plans that I have for you,' declares the LORD, 'plans for welfare and not for calamity to give you a future and a hope'" (Jeremiah 29:11; see also Nahum 1:7; Romans 8:28).

» God is sufficient for all our needs. "Not that

we are adequate in ourselves to consider anything as coming from ourselves, but our adequacy is from God" (2 Corinthians 3:5; 1 Corinthians 15:10; Proverbs 21:1).

- God will never leave us or forsake us. "Be strong and courageous, do not be afraid or tremble at them, for the LORD your God is the one who goes with you. He will not fail you or forsake you" (Deuteronomy 31:6).
- God can be trusted to keep his Word. "Jesus Christ is the same yesterday and today and forever" (Hebrews 13:8).
- We can trust him. "In God I have put my trust, I shall not be afraid. What can man do to me?" (Psalm 56:11; 91:2; 118:8; Isaiah 26:3-4).

This is our hope! Perhaps you are a helping friend, counselor, mentor, or just a good listener; if so you may encourage a hurting wife by seeking to introduce her to a loving and caring God whom she may know in a personal way. This precious, loving God gave his life on the cross for her and rose from the grave three days later to give her new life. As she walks along her journey, we can show her how to seek him, who endured the cross, despising the shame (Hebrews 12:2). He knows how we feel—and leads us to joy.

> *For we do not have a high priest who*
> *cannot sympathize with our weaknesses,*
> *but One who has been tempted*
> *in all things as we are, yet without*
> *sin. Therefore let us draw near with*
> *confidence to the throne of grace, so that*
> *we may receive mercy and find grace to*
> *help in time of need.*
>
> (Hebrews 4:15–16)

People will always let us down. God never will. When we trust the Lord it is as if he is carrying us on his wings.

> *As an eagle stirreth up her nest, fluttereth*
> *over her young, spreadeth abroad her*
> *wings, taketh them, beareth them on her*
> *wings: So the* LORD *...*
>
> (Deuteronomy 32:11, KJV)

There is a story of a mother eagle who was enticing her little one to trust her and fly. As he was looking down, unwilling to attempt it, she rose high above him, giving a sharp cry that made him alert and tense as a watch-spring. In an instant the mother eagle had swooped, striking the nest at his feet, sending him into the air.

As he flapped lustily for life, she was over him, under him, beside him, hovering tirelessly, calling softly that she was there. But his flapping grew wilder and he fell faster and faster. Soon he lost his strength and stopped his flapping and was heading downwards headfirst, to be dashed into pieces. It was over for him.

Then, like a flash, the mother eagle shot under him; his despairing feet touched her broad shoulders between her wings. He righted himself, rested an instant, and found his head; then she dropped like a shot from under him, leaving him to come down on his own wings. In this manner she taught her eaglet to fly.[9]

Oh, hurting friend, there is great hope as you get to know God and learn to trust him with your life!

My prayer is that, if you are struggling with submission, if you are being abused, or if you need help, you will go to your local church and seek guidance and refuge in a safe place. It is also my prayer that through the stories and Scriptures in this book you will have received some insight that God offers hope. God does care.

Your story may not be like those mentioned, but God's Word says in Ecclesiastes that there is nothing new under the sun. God understands your situation, and it is not his desire that you should suffer wrong from another person, especially your husband. God will carry you through.

One day, we who know Jesus will be in God's kingdom and there will be no more pain. In the meantime, let us be found faithful, living in obedience to the command he has given us to submit to our husbands, for

> *All Scripture is inspired by God and*
> *profitable for teaching, for reproof, for*
> *correction, for training in righteousness;*
> *so that the man [or woman] of God*
> *may be adequate, equipped for every*
> *good work.*
>
> (2 Timothy 3:16–17)

Conclusion

If you find yourself in a place similar to the women in the true stories in this book, please don't judge them. They are each accepting their roles as submissive wives and learning to adjust, to fit into their husbands' ways. Each woman's situation is different, yet Scripture offers hope for us all.

It is as we walk closely with our Lord and Savior that we will hold our heads high and know that we can submit, not because our sinner-man deserves it or because we want to, but because his Spirit enables us to. He will take care of us—as on the wings of an eagle.

We are bombarded on every side with newspapers, books, magazines, and other media saying, "Do your own thing," "You deserve a break today," "Have it your way." We need to encourage one another toward love and good works.

And let us consider how to stimulate one

another to love and good deeds.

(Hebrews 10:24)

But I say, walk by the Spirit, and you will not carry out the desire of the flesh. For the flesh sets its desire against the Spirit, and the Spirit against the flesh; for these are in opposition to one another, so that you may not do the things that you please.

(Galatians 5:16–17)

I leave you with the words of Carolyn McCulley, a speaker and author from the True Woman Conference,[10] as she tells of her journey out of the world's feminism and into preparation for submission in marriage.[11]

Though I felt God was calling me [as a new believer] to this church, I was in for a culture shock! It was like being on another planet—the women and their viewpoints there were completely foreign to me. I remember meeting with my pastor and his wife shortly after I started attending and making a crack about submission. I did not think anyone still believed that part of the Bible! My pastor wisely asked me if I liked to read and then recommended Recovering Biblical Manhood and Womanhood[12] *to me—theological reading not typically recommended to a two-month-old convert.*

The Lord used that conversation to start retooling my concept of femininity and sexuality, overhauling my lifelong views on abortion, sexual immorality, and even submission. I read God's Word, hungry to find out why my new church friends held views so different from anyone else I knew. From Genesis, I came to understand that God is purposeful in his creation. From the Gospels, I came to understand that God is purposeful in his redemption. I saw he was quite serious about sexual purity before marriage and fidelity within marriage. I was also convicted that abortion was a terribly selfish action to avoid the consequences of sexual sin.

Just as importantly, I saw that God had made me female, and that he had specific tasks and roles for women that would glorify him to an unbelieving, yet watching, world. Slowly, I was becoming more concerned with his glory and not my own.

As I studied the Bible, I also studied the marriages of my new friends eager to see what this Christian concept of benevolent masculine leadership and joyful feminine submission actually looked like in real life. Though not perfect, what I saw was attractive. I saw men who sacrificed their own preferences and pleasures to make sure their wives and children were cultivated spiritually. These were men who took their responsibilities to be servant leaders seriously. They did not see marriage as a trap or children as an impediment to the pursuit of their own leisure and weekend hobbies. Instead, their families were seen as gifts worthy of their hard work.

Likewise, I saw that my married women's friends sought to respect and build up their husbands. I was used to a stream of cracks from women about the uselessness and unreliability of men, but this I did not hear from the mature, married women in my church. Their submission seemed freeing ... dare I say, liberating*?! They certainly seemed free from much of the discord, sarcasm, and disappointment I usually encountered in modern marriages.*

Slowly I began to note that the teamwork in these marriages mirrored the teamwork in the church. While married men had the responsibility of leading their families, these same men were called to submit to the spiritual leaders God had put over them. In fact, when I was focused on the "limitations" I perceived in a wife's submission to her husband, I showed that I had failed to understand that submission undergirds the entire concept of Christianity. My greatest role model for submission is my Lord himself whose obedient submission guaranteed my redemption. As Heb-

rews 5:7 says, "During the days of Jesus' life on earth, he offered up prayers and petitions with loud cries and tears to the one who could save him from death, and he was heard because of his reverent submission" [NIV].

Over time, as I grew to know the Lord and his Word better, I realized that the independence I had worked so hard to protect as an unbeliever was a complete charade. As a helpless, finite creature, I was completely dependent on God for my very life and breath. I had not been independent. Rather, I had been stiff-necked. I came to realize that submission simply stripped me of my contentiousness, not my dignity as one created in the very image of God ...

Paul urged the Galatians to remember that "it is for freedom that Christ has set us free." Prior to my conversion, I saw Christianity as being a burden, a confining religion with many rules and regulations. I was not equipped to see that my own sin was the greatest yoke of slavery. As we have all done since Adam and Eve, I blamed others for the oppression of sin in my life. I thought I needed to be set free from men who belittled women, from jobs that were "stuck" in the "pink ghetto" of women's work, and from the "burdens" of traditional sexual morals. I could not see that my own self-righteousness, pride, anger, and willfulness caused greater damage to real joy than any perceived curtailment to my freedom.

When Christ ushered in his kingdom, he surprised everyone—including his own disciples—with the "opposite world" that he introduced. Everything was "backward" to the natural thinking of human beings. The greatest among us were servants. Our enemies were to be prayed for and even loved. What makes us unclean comes from inside of us, in our hearts, not from what we put on or in us. To have life everlasting, we must be born again.

It does not make sense on first reading, but the Bible promises us that God's wisdom is foolishness to a perishing world (1 Corinthians 1:18–21). I am just most grateful that he liberated me from my futile thinking and the bondage of sin and led me into the way everlasting.[13]

May all of us wives be so liberated as we live out our godly role of submission to our own husbands!

> For it is God who is at work in you, both
> to will and to work for His good pleasure.
> (Philippians 2:13)

Personal Application Projects

1. Read about Abigail in 1 Samuel 25 and look for the ways she planned her appeal to two difficult men. Consider her approach. What was so special about Abigail that she was called the woman with beauty and brains ("intelligent and beautiful in appearance")? Can you see any application from Abigail for your situation?
2. Study 1 Peter 3:1-6.
    - » What does Peter mean when he says that the disobedient husband may be "won without a word"?
    - » What is "chaste and respectful behavior"?
    - » Though a wife's care for, and beautifying of, her outward appearance is one means of honoring and loving her husband, these verses teach that the "hidden person" is to be the higher priority. Why?
    - » How can you follow Sarah's example?
    - » What does Peter mean when he says that

the godly wife can live "without ... fear"?

» What changes does the Lord want you to make as a result of studying this passage of Scripture?

3. Titus 2:3–5 says that older women are to teach the younger. There is always someone older than you. Would you be willing to seek out an older woman and ask her to meet with you to answer questions you have regarding submission? Look for someone who has a reputation for being a godly woman, one whose life you've watched and whom you have seen acting out her submission to her husband. Allow another woman to encourage you through the learning process. If this scares you a little, remember it can be for a brief time until you get some confidence in discerning for yourself.
4. Consider a few practical things to help you grow:

   » Read God's Word daily and jot down a few words or phrases in a journal about what you are learning.

   » Attend a local church weekly. You cannot grow in isolation. You will meet others to share life with and enjoy friendships, and you will learn how others apply God's Word to their lives.

» Join a women's Bible study, do the assignments, and interact with the others in your group. It will be helpful for you to hear how other godly women handle submission. Others are going through similar struggles and you can encourage one another.

» Last but not least, pray daily. Learn to pray without ceasing. Pray for your husband. Pray about your husband. Pray for yourself and your attitude.

These few things can help you to become faithful in your journey in submission.

5. Finally, develop good communication skills. Go back to the basics. You will want to give your facts, thoughts, ideas, intuitions, and opinions—not your feelings. As a general rule, men think more than they feel. Consider writing what you want to say in your journal. Write as much as you want to say and all the feelings you need to express. Then go back with a highlighter and cross out what isn't

necessary. Then go back and do it again. End up with a very concise presentation of what is really important for him to know. Wait until after dinner or after the children have gone to bed or while you are out walking together when things are good between you. When I communicate with my husband, I need to use small sound bites, a time frame, think what my expectations are from him (Will he need to fix it? And if so, when?), and basic communication guidelines (i.e. "I have something to say. It will take three minutes. Is now a good time?"). Maybe it will be similar with your husband. Get to know what you need to do to most effectively communicate your concerns to your husband.

What would you like to tell your husband today? If you are prepared, you will be ready when the right time comes.

May God bless you as you strive to walk in a manner that is pleasing unto your Lord.

I will be praying for you.

Where Can I Get More Help?

Books

John S. Barnett, *Discipline Yourself for Godliness* (Tulsa, OK: Mullerhaus, 2007)

John S. Barnett, *The Joy of the Word-Filled Family* (Tulsa, OK: Mullerhaus, 2004)

Jerry Bridges, *Trusting God: Even When Life Hurts* (Colorado Springs: NavPress, 1988)

C. Cowman, *Streams in the Desert*, Vol. 2. (Grand Rapids, MI: Zondervan, 1996)

Nancy DeMoss, *Lies Women Believe and the Truth That Sets Them Free* (Chicago: Moody, 2001)

Elizabeth Rice Handford, *Me? Obey Him?* (Murfreesboro, TN: Word of the Lord, 1972)

Herbert Lockyer, *All the Women of the Bible* (Grand Rapids, MI: Zondervan, 1967)

Dorothy McGuire, Carol Lewis, and Alvena Blatchley, *Submission: Are There Limits?* (Denver, CO: TRI-R Ministries, 1992)

John Piper, "The Beautiful Faith of Fearless Submission," April 15, 2007, sermon available at www.desiringgod.org/

Alexander Strauch, *Men and Women, Equal Yet Different* (Colorado Springs: Lewis & Roth 1999)

Web Sites and Other Media

The True Woman Movement: www.truewoman.com

Mary Kassian, 'You've Come a Long Way, Baby!', October 10, 2008, message at True Woman Conference Chicago 2008; watch, listen, or read the message under 'Media & Articles' at www.truewoman.com.

The author's Web site: www.glendahotton.com. Follow the link to the "Brides" section.

End Notes

1. The survey participants are identified only by their initials.
2. Titus Two Bible study groups are based on Titus 2:3–5: "Older women ... are to ... encourage the young women to love their husbands, to love their children, to be sensible, pure, workers at home, kind, being subject to their own husbands, so that the word of God will not be dishonored."
3. All names have been changed to protect the identities of those involved.
4. Jim Newheiser, *HELP! Someone I Love Has Been Abused* (Wapwallopen, PA: Shepherd Press, 2014), 28.
5. U.S. Census Bureau, "Marriage and Divorce," www.census.gov/hhes/socdemo/marriage/index.html.
6. Dorothy McGuire, Carol Lewis, and Alvena Blatchley, *Submission: Are There Limits?* (Colorado: TRI-R Ministries, 1992), 29.
7. Fanny J. Crosby, "Blessed Assurance," 1873.
8. Based on Herbert Lockyer, *All the Women of the Bible* (Grand Rapids, MI: Zondervan, 1967), 23–25.
9. Christabel Gladwell, January 26, in C. Cowman, *Streams in the Desert*, Vol. 2 (Grand Rapids, MI: Zondervan, 1996).
10. See www.truewoman.com/.
11. This text is reproduced with the author's permission.
12. John Piper and Wayne Grudem, (eds.), *Recovering Biblical Manhood and Womanhood* (Wheaton, IL: Crossway, 1991).
13. From www.truewoman.com/; accessed March 11, 2011.

Books in the Help! series include...

- Help! He's Struggling with Pornography
- Help! Someone I Love Has Been Abused
- Help! My Toddler Rules the House
- Help! Someone I Love Has Cancer
- Help! I Want to Change
- Help! My Spouse Has Been Unfaithful
- Help! Someone I Love Has Alzheimer's
- Help! I Have Breast Cancer
- Help! I'm a Slave to Food
- Help! My Teen Struggles With Same-Sex Attractions
- Help! She's Struggling With Pornography
- Help! I Can't Get Motivated
- Help! I'm a Single Mom
- Help! I'm Confused About Dating
- Help! I'm Drowning in Debt
- Help! My Teen is Rebellious
- Help! I'm Depressed
- Help! I'm Living With Terminal Illness
- Help! I Feel Ashamed
- Help! I Want to Model Submission in Marriage
- Help! I Can't Handle All These Trials
- Help! I Can't Forgive
- Help! My Anger is Out of Control
- Help! My Friend is Suicidal
- Help! I'm in a Conflict
- Help! I'm Being Deployed
- Help! I've Been Traumatized by Combat
- Help! I'm So Lonely
- Help! My Kids Are Viewing Pornography
- Help! I Need a Church

More titles in preparation

For current listing go to: www.shepherdpress.com/lifeline

About Shepherd Press Publications

- » They are gospel driven.
- » They are heart focused.
- » They are life changing.

Our Invitation to You

We passionately believe that what we are publishing can be of benefit to you, your family, your friends, and your work colleagues. So we are inviting you to join our online mailing list so that we may reach out to you with news about our latest and forthcoming publications, and with special offers.

Visit:

www.shepherdpress.com/newsletter

and provide your name and email address.